We miss y.

Pauline, [?] C, Emily

The Little Gift Book of

WASHINGTON

The Little Gift Book of

WASHINGTON

Whitecap Books
Vancouver / Toronto

Copyright © 1991 by Whitecap Books
Whitecap Books
Vancouver/Toronto

Fourth Printing, 1998

Text by Elaine Jones
Edited by Linda Ostrowalker
Cover and Interior design by Steve Penner
Typography by CompuType, Vancouver, B.C., Canada

Printed and bound in Canada by Friesen Printers,
    Altona, Manitoba

Canadian Cataloguing in Publication Data
    Jones, Elaine.
        The little gift book of Washington

    ISBN 1-895099-37-4

    1. Washington (State) — Description and
travel — 1981 — Views. I. Title.
F892.J65 1991   979.7'043'0222   C91-091046-4

Contents

Wheat field near Steptoe Butte.

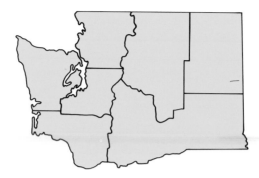

Washington

The first thing to know about Washington is that it is impossible to characterize in a few words. This diverse state has a range of climate, topography, communities, activities and occupations that is unrivalled among all the states.

Located in the northwest corner of the country, it is bordered to the east by Idaho and to the south by Oregon. Within its 68,000-square-mile area are open ocean and protected seashores, dense forests, arid desert areas with dry canyons, sand dunes and mesas, powerful rivers, mountains and rolling plains. The natural features of the state — the ocean, the Columbia River and its basin, and the mountains — provide the framework for this land of contrasts.

To the west is the wide open Pacific. But Washington also boasts Puget Sound, one of the world's most remarkable inland seas, an extensive inlet that winds for some one hundred miles among myriad coves, bays and islands, surrounded to both west and east by two magnificent mountain ranges: the Olympics and the Cascades.

The Cascades are the backbone of Washington. This range forms part of a continuous chain of mountains that extends from Mexico to Alaska.

Left: *Seattle at night.*

It is due to their presence that the state can boast both lush overgrown rainforests and sand dunes.

The Cascades are from fifty to a hundred miles in width. On the wet, Pacific side, heavy rainfall and a temperate climate moderated by a warm ocean current encourage lush vegetation. Here the commercial fishing industry, the forest industries and tourism take advantage of this natural bounty. To the east, on the dry, lee side of the Cascades, the luxuriant rainforest gives way to open pine woods and eventually the flat plains of the interior and the arid center of the state. The climate changes dramatically, and long, hot summers, cold winters and the fertile Columbia Basin promote an agricultural industry that has grown to include not just grains and vegetables, but fruit and wine production. In the northeast corner of the state rise the Okanagan Highlands and the Selkirk Mountains, minor divisions of the Rocky Mountains.

Much of Washington's natural beauty is protected in national and state parks and forests, and these areas are a mecca for travellers in all seasons — backpacking, hiking, skiing, water activities, and simply enjoying unparalleled scenic beauty.

Marking Washington's southern boundary and traversing its interior plateau is the mighty Columbia River. The river has played a central role in the development of the state. Its passage through the Cascades, carved out as the mountains were forming, was a highway for native peoples and the route of European exploration; today it is still a busy commercial waterway and its five great dams provide hydroelectric power and irrigation for the rich soil of the Columbia Basin.

The communities of Washington are also diverse. They range from the state capital, Olympia, with its gracious tree-lined streets, to the sophistication of Seattle, Bellevue, Tacoma and the picturesque coastal villages and robust farming and ranching communities, and they draw on a wide range of cultural backgrounds.

Washington's state motto is "Al-ki," Chinook for "by and by," and this phrase perhaps typifies the relaxed friendly neighborliness of the people here. For the visitor who finds the variety of things to do and startling regional contrasts a little overwhelming at first, it might be well to adopt this motto. Exploring Washington a little at a time, area by area, "by and by" the whole of this fascinating state can be discovered.

Long Beach near Cape Disappointment.

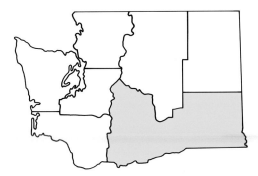

The Southeast

The Southeast part of Washington comprises vast empty spaces, a rugged mountain wilderness, rolling fields of wheat and other crops, ordered, comfortable river valleys that produce a heady crop of grapes, and well-established historic communities strung out along the rivers.

This is big country, and it is traversed by two mighty rivers: the Columbia and the Snake. Much of the history of the region can be found along these two rivers, the route taken by Lewis and Clark on their great inland expedition. Points of interest along the route are marked for travellers all the way from Clarkston to Ilwaco on the west coast.

While the Snake River is not as voluminous as the Columbia (it is ranked sixth in the United States), the Snake has its own unique beauty as it winds through the mesas and canyons of southeast Washington. From Clarkston, it's possible to travel upriver to the famed Hell's Canyon in Oregon. To the west, scenic attractions along the Snake River— the most impressive being the 2000-foot vertical canyon walls carved by the river — are available to boaters between Clarkston and Lower Granite Dam.

South of the Snake River lie the Blue Mountains, true to their name rising

Left: *Wheat field in Whitman County.*

7

from the basalt plains in a blue haze. Part of the Umatilla National Forest, the Blue Mountains are an almost treeless wilderness. Today they are crossed by trails for hikers and horseback riders, and facilities include campsites and a downhill ski area, but peaks such as Mount Misery and Mount Horrible suggest that the remote area was not always viewed so favorably.

West of here, Walla Walla is the center of an agricultural district extending north to Dayton and west to the Tri-Cities. The area produces many different crops but Walla Walla is famed for its mild, sweet onions — celebrated with an annual festival.

The character of the Columbia River through the southeast portion of the state is very different from its western portion. East of the Cascades the basalt cliffs of the Columbia Plateau are topped with rolling grasslands. Settlements are sparse upstream from the Tri-Cities.

Pasco, Kennewick and Richland, at the confluence of the Snake and the Columbia rivers, enjoy the twin benefits of great water resources and a climate that provides nonstop sun for well over half the year. Pasco, established in 1884, is the oldest of the three communities. The development of the Hanford Atomic Energy Works in the 1940s gave a boost to the development of the area, vastly expanding Richland and neighboring Kennewick. Despite the abundance of water at the Tri-Cities, it is just a short jaunt — eight miles from Pasco — to a 7000-acre desert of sand dunes and juniper at Juniper Dunes Wilderness.

Wineries and expansive farms surround the Tri-Cities and the string of small communities along the Yakima River. Rich volcanic soil and irrigation have combined to create a flourishing wine industry, as well as growing a variety of fruits, vegetables and hops. Frequent roadside stands testify to the bounty of the harvest. At Ellensburg, the ranching history of the area is preserved in restored buildings and museums, but also in a living way, with the Ellensburg Rodeo — the largest in the state.

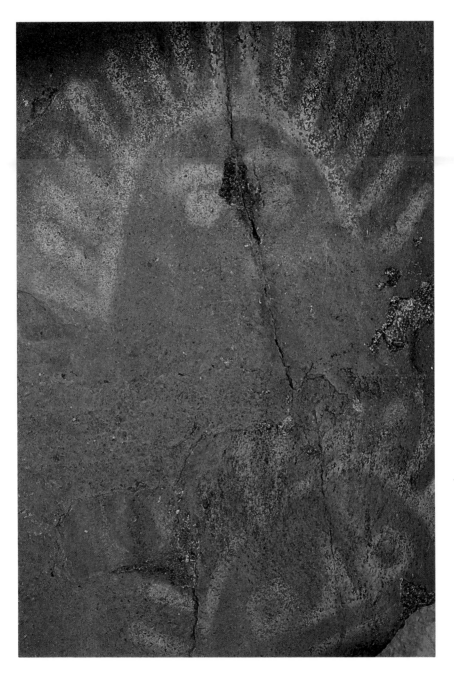

Petroglyphs near Yakima.

Main administration building,
Washington State University in Pullman.

Stonehenge replica built by the late
Sam Hill of Goldendale.

Palouse Falls.

Yakima River Valley.

Zinnia field near Othello.

Fishing on Dog Lake.

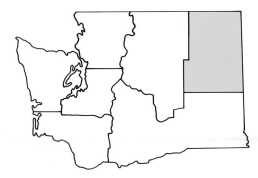

The Northeast

The northeast section of the state contains Washington's largest lake, expansive farmlands to the south and the almost uninhabited northeast corner. The relatively unexplored but impressive Colville and Kaniksu national forests include the wilderness of the Kettle Mountains, where Washington's highest mountain pass, 5575-foot Sherman Pass, connects Republic and Kettle Falls. The hub for this diversity is Spokane.

Spokane is Washington's second-largest city, a pleasant, welcoming community that is known for its many fine parks and golf courses. Far from the seaports, with their constant flux of international commerce, Spokane developed quietly as the center of a prosperous agricultural area known as the "Inland Empire." The city grew up around the Spokane River, incorporating its impressive series of falls into the downtown area with Riverfront Park. Over the years, agriculture has widened to include wine-making; several wineries in the Spokane area offer wine-tasting tours. Mining and logging have also been important here and, once off the efficient main highways, a backroads explorer can discover gold-mining towns interspersed with vast farms.

Left: *Rock sculptures, Bridge Creek Road near Inchelium.*

West of Spokane, the small community of Odessa is representative of the spirit of the farming communities here. Its Odessa Fest celebrates the German heritage, attracting thousands of visitors each year to this town of 2000 residents. North of here, the Hutterite community of Marlin offers the public a glimpse into the heritage of this sect.

Although Washington has natural wonders in abundance, its manmade features sometimes equal what nature has provided. The state's largest lake, Franklin Roosevelt Lake, was created with construction of the Grand Coulee Dam. Essentially a widening of the Columbia River, it extends 120 miles upstream from the dam. The lake has become a popular recreational resource, with several campgrounds and resorts along its 630-mile shoreline. The waters offer excellent fishing and opportunities for swimming, exploring or simply enjoying the scenery.

On Lake Roosevelt's south shore, Fort Spokane's historic buildings tell of the time around 1880 when the fort was built to keep peace between settlers and native Indians.

The lake roughly bisects the Colville National Forest and Kaniksu National Forest. This is rugged backcountry that appeals to wilderness explorers and fishing enthusiasts — virtually all of the myriad lakes and streams are excellent trout-fishing waters. There is also a well-used downhill ski area east of Chewelah. For the history buff or backroads explorer, these mountains hold another treasure: ghost towns and remains of the gold-mining boom days are scattered along disused roads. Streambeds will also yield an occasional nugget to determined gold-panners.

Republic was built on the gold rush of 1896, and is the only historic gold mining town in this area to have survived. Republic also offers a taste of the more remote past — from 47 million years ago — at the Stonerose Interpretive Center. Embedded in the rocks here are fossils from the Eocene Epoch.

Wheat fields south of Spokane.

Spokane skyline.

Franklin Roosevelt Lake
formed by Grand Coulee Dam.

Ione Chamber of Commerce
visitors' booth.

Cathedral of St. John the Evangelist.

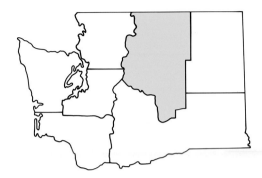

North-Central Washington

The north central area of Washington encompasses a number of impressive natural features, including the eastern slopes of the Cascades, Lake Chelan and Dry Falls, but perhaps the biggest attraction here is manmade: the Grand Coulee Dam.

Not only was the dam a stupendous engineering task, it is the major link in a system that irrigates some 2 million acres of formerly arid land in the Columbia Basin and incidentally provides some of the best-used recreational sites in the state. A magnificent example of cooperation between man and nature, it harnesses the awesome power of the Columbia River in one of the largest hydroelectric concrete structures in the world: 5,233 feet long (about twelve city blocks) and 555 feet tall. Self-guided tours cross the top of the main dam and enter the interior. At night a laser and sound show illuminates the spillway and the water cascading over it. Behind the dam, Banks Lake occupies a natural reservoir left dry when the ancient glacial riverbed changed course. Boating and fishing are popular activities on this waterway, which has a good supply of trout.

East of the Cascades is the Columbia Plateau, traversed by the "big

Left: *Grand Coulee Dam.*

bend" of the Columbia and characterized by dry coulees and canyons, remnants of the ice age. The most spectacular of these is Dry Falls, a three-mile-wide relic of the ice-age Columbia River. Here the river took a 400-foot plunge over the lip to the deep channel called Lower Grand Coulee. But this dry, sun-drenched land is also blessed with plenty of water in surprising places, thanks to the overflow from dam reservoirs. Sun Lakes State Park encompasses the twenty-mile chain of small, trout-stocked lakes in Lower Grand Coulee, and is one of the most-visited parks in the state. Just south of Moses Lake, seepage from the reservoirs of irrigation projects has created another surprise among the sand dunes. Potholes Reservoir State Park comprises fifty reservoirs that are stocked with trout, perch and bass.

Fertile river valleys — the Columbia and its tributaries: Wenatchee, Methow and Okanagan — provide soil and water for a thriving orchard industry, and the radiant sunshine does the rest. In the summer, just-picked produce is always available from the many fruit stands along the highways.

The major center in this region is Wenatchee, dubbed the apple capital of the state and centrally located for access to both the mountainous recreational areas and the lakes and streams of the south coulee area, from Banks Lake to Potholes Reservoir.

Fifty-five-mile-long Lake Chelan is one of Washington's largest lakes and perhaps best exemplifies the contrasts found in this part of the state. Its southern end, complete with a full range of resorts and facilities, lies in rolling, sun-baked hills bordering the Columbia Plateau; at the northern end is Stehekin, which is reachable by boat and it the base for hiking and camping in the heavily forested wilderness of North Cascades National Park. A boat trip on the *Lady of the Lake* takes visitors on a one-day round trip cruise to enjoy the dramatic change in scenery, or drops them off at Stehekin for trips on foot into the park.

Apples at Wenatchee.

*Western-style town of Winthrop,
northern Cascades.*

Early Winters Spires,
summit of Washington Pass.

Chief Joseph's gravesite.

Wheat fields near Coulee City.

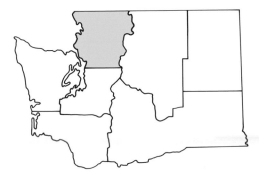

The Northwest

A stranger to the northwest corner of Washington may well wonder in which direction to travel. On the west is one of the best boating areas in the United States, the incomparable San Juan archipelago, comprising 172 islands. A very pleasant drive to the east, through forests and farmlands, are the Cascade Mountains, the jagged, northern portion of which is set aside in North Cascades National park. A meander down the coastline yields spectacular views of Puget Sound and the San Juan Islands, as well as a series of charming communities.

The Cascades are known for their major volcanic mountains and this part of the state is dominated by Mount Baker. Its symmetrical, snow-shrouded form is visible for miles, seeming to hover magically above the horizon from as far away as British Columbia. One of the giants of the Cascades at 10,750 feet, the perpetually snow-clad peak is the center of a year-round recreational area.

The San Juan archipelago is a fascinating combination of fishing communities, tiny hamlets that thrive on summer's influx of visitors and an intricate coastline that tempts visitors with new vistas at every turn. Its

Left: *Sailboats at Semiahmoo Bay.*

temperate climate is ideal for all outdoor activities, especially boating, fishing, biking and camping. Its waters teem with marine life — the fishing is great for salmon and halibut, the shellfish are bountiful and there are opportunities to catch sight of killer whales or dolphins sporting in the water. An excellent ferry fleet makes many of the islands available to the car traveller; others, to the great pleasure of boaters, remain water accessible only.

Aside from the recreational pleasures afforded by the islands, the San Juans are notable for their history and culture. San Juan and Orcas islands have thriving centers for the performing arts. San Juan is also the site of the 1859 "Pig War." Ostensibly begun over the theft of a pig, British and American forces both laid claim to the territory. A peaceful war, both sides socialized regularly until the dispute was resolved in 1872. The fortifications are still visible at either end of the island and have been made into a two-part National Historic Park.

Deception Pass State Park, on the north end of Whidbey Island, is an area of exceptional scenic beauty and one of Washington's most popular parks. Divers and others are drawn to the dramatic tidal rapids at the narrows of Deception Pass, where a bridge connects sixty-mile-long Whidbey Island to the mainland; a ferry operates from the south end. Whidbey Island is also the site of Fort Casey, a Second World War naval base now dedicated as a park. Several links connect Whidbey, Fidalgo and Camano islands to the nearby mainland, yet they retain that special island quality, where time seems to have stopped and quiet seaside towns seem largely unchanged for the past century.

Everett and Bellingham are the two main centers in this part of the state. Between them is a scenic highway dotted with many interesting stops. La Conner, one of Washington's oldest towns, boasts 161 historic buildings, shops and working canneries. Further north, picturesque Chuckanut Drive runs for ten of its twenty miles close to the shore through Larrabee State Park.

Daffodil fields near La Conner.

Downhill skiing on Mt. Baker.

Falls in Mt. Baker National Forest.

View from the Sahale Glacier,
north Cascades.

Mt. Baker summit.

La Conner during tulip festival.

Horses near Rockport.

Barn in Skagit County.

San Juan Islands.

*Puget Sound with Olympic Mountains
in background.*

Reaching the top, Sahale Glacier.

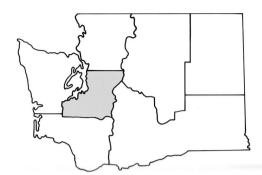

King County and South Puget Sound

Bordering the scenic Puget Sound area is the densest population cluster in the state, containing the almost continuous populations of Bellevue, Seattle, Tacoma and the state capital, Olympia. Yet just a short distance away are the Cascades and towering Mount Rainier — the high point of the Cascades at 14,410 feet. The national park surrounding this peak is one of the state's most popular destinations, appealing to a wide range of travellers, from backpackers to those touring by vehicle.

Seattle has come a long way from its rough and tumble beginnings. From the time that the first ship docked here laden with gold ore from the Yukon, Seattle has based its rapid and continuing growth on its port facilities. Today it is a cosmopolitan city of over 1.5 million people and its harbor is not only a workplace but a major recreational attraction. The harbor is in two main parts: modern port facilities that efficiently process oceangoing container ships and the old working harbor, with the Pike Place Market adjacent, offering fresh produce, imported and handcrafted items and eating

Left: *Seattle with Mount Rainier in the background.*

establishments varying from takeout to gourmet (naturally featuring daily-fresh seafood). A thriving International District south of the city center and the 74-acre Seattle Center, created after the 1962 World's Fair and featuring the 605-foot Space Needle, are just two more of Seattle's many attractions.

Tacoma, its city center thirty-five miles south of Seattle, was founded in 1840. It got its start as the terminus of a transcontinental railway, thus launching a rivalry with Seattle that continues in a friendly fashion between the sister cities. Tacoma is a jumping-off point for both Puget Sound and Mount Rainier National Park.

Mount Rainier National Park is one of three national parks in Washington. Dominated by the dormant volcanic cone of Mount Rainier, it encompasses almost 242,000 acres of spectacular wilderness — alpine meadows and mountain lakes and streams, virgin forests, a network of trails for every level of ability, ice caves and spectacular glaciers that radiate like spokes from the peak. Not only does the park support a variety of environments, it harbors many forms of wildlife, from beaver, squirrels, snowshoe hares, hawks and other bird life, to larger mammals such as black bears, mountain goats, deer and elk.

Olympia, the state capital, is located at the southernmost extension of Puget Sound. The abundant and delicious oysters of local bays have become a trademark of gourmet restaurants in the area. Many fine public buildings and museums, including the capital buildings and their fifty-five acres of grounds — thought to be some of the most beautiful in the country — lend an air of grace to the city.

The cities of the coast revel in their situation on beautiful Puget Sound. Often fogbound in winter, the area is glorious in the summer months, when day after day of sunshine tempered by cool ocean breezes create an idyllic environment, and a perfect getaway from city life.

Wildflowers on Mt. Rainier.

Legislative Buildings, Olympia.

Indian totem.

War memorial, Olympia.

*Pike Place Market, a favorite for
tourists and locals alike.*

Elliott Bay, Puget Sound.

Temple of Justice, Olympia.

Seattle skyline.

Trail riding, Mt. Rainier National Park.

Budd Canal, Olympia.

Boeing Museum, Seattle.

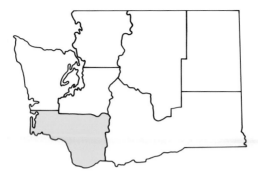

The Southwest

The southwest corner of Washington is distinguished by extremes, and yet it has a gentle aura permeated with the past. It has the longest sandy beach in North America, the continent's most powerful river — the Columbia — and Mount St. Helens, the most serene of the volcanic peaks in the Cascades until the top blew off in an awesome display of nature's power. The site is now a National Volcanic Monument of 110,000 acres.

The southwest region is rich in history. Its southern border with Oregon is formed by the Columbia River, the highway to early exploration. This has always been the busiest part of the river; highways parallel both sides and the river bustles with the commerce of shipping and fishing. Evidence of the early explorers and fortifications of the Hudson's Bay Company can be found here as well; history seekers can begin their own explorations with the interpretive center at Cape Disappointment, which details the journey of Lewis and Clark. One of Washington's landmarks is 858-foot-tall Beacon Rock — the world's second-largest monolith — where Lewis and Clark first detected the effects of the tides on their journey of discovery down the Columbia.

Left: *Spirit Lake, Mount St. Helens.*

Vancouver is Washington's oldest city and there is ample evidence of its historic past. Fort Vancouver was a Hudson's Bay trading post and an authentically restored stockade and five major buildings dating from 1850 form a vignette of pioneer life. Officer's Row is a group of homes built between 1849 and 1906; one of the houses is a museum dedicated to Ulysses S. Grant, who was stationed here as a young officer.

On the Pacific is Long Beach, a narrow, low-lying peninsula twenty-eight miles long. The sandy spit has been a resort retreat for a century; today the shingled cottages of previous generations share space with luxurious new resorts. Along its length, a number of communities — such as Ilwaco, Nahcotta and Oysterville — typify west coast fishing communities and the maritime tradition of the area. Oysterville, true to its name, is an oystering community that dates from 1854, now designated a national historic district.

Centralia and Chehalis are the centers for the dairying and logging industries of the Cowlitz Plain. The White Pass Highway connects Chehalis with Yakima via one of the four mountain passes that connect eastern and western Washington across the barrier of the Cascades.

The eastern part of the region is taken up with the Cascade Mountains. Despite massive Mount Adams, the second tallest peak in the range, and the eruption of Mount St. Helens, the Cascades here have a gentler aspect than the northern part of the chain. The climate is warmer and drier, access is easier, partly due to an extensive network of logging roads, and there are many day hikes available. Gifford Pinchot National Forest encompasses the full range of wilderness experiences available here — from second-growth forests to wilderness preserves, from gentle slopes to the craggy peaks of the Goat Rocks, and from the new life emerging from the ash of Mount St. Helens to the ancient forests of Mount Adams.

*Inside lighthouse at
Cape Disappointment.*

Covered bridge near Rosburg.

Windsurfing on Columbia River at Cook.

Vents on Mount St. Helens.

Sunflower near Cougar.

Grassy field, Leadbetter Point.

*Langfield Falls in Gifford Pinchot
National Forest.*

Sunset on the Columbia.

Mt. Adams.

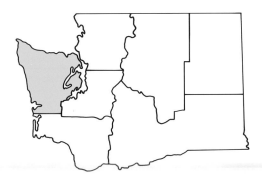

The Olympic Peninsula

Washington's Olympic Peninsula is almost a separate continent, complete with ocean, lakes and rivers, and its own mountain range. Fronting on the open Pacific and framed to the north by the Strait of Juan de Fuca, its protected eastern shore is formed by the deep indentation of Puget Sound. The grand Olympic Mountains claim the major portion of the peninsula, rising in magnificent snow-capped peaks.

Dominated by these mountains, much of the peninsula has a remote feeling and has become a favorite destination for wilderness trekkers. The Olympic National Park and Forest preserve nearly a million acres of pristine forest, including the entire Olympic Range and a narrow strip of coastline. While much of it is best experienced by hiking in from the roadways, there are some magnificent areas that are accessible to day-trippers, such as 5200-foot-high Hurricane Ridge, which offers panoramic views just a twenty-minute drive from Port Angeles. From Quinault, on the shores of Lake Quinault, there is access to the three lush river valleys of the range: the Quinault, the Queets, and the Hoh.

Most of the peninsula remains lightly populated, the communities clus-

Left: *Sailboats in Port Townsend.*

tering at the northeast corner and to the south. Along the protected eastern shore, the Hood Canal shoreline offers excellent parks to enjoy the bays and coves and harvest the abundant shellfish available on the beaches. Colorful villages provide a break from the grandeur of the environment.

The Kitsap Peninsula is a convoluted assortment of bays and coves anchored to the main Olympic Peninsula by a narrow neck of land. It can also be reached via the Narrows Bridge at Tacoma or ferry from Seattle. Bremerton is the largest community, but nearby there is an interesting cross-section of lumbering and fishing villages. State and county parks, as well as private enterprises, offer access to the virtually limitless activities of Puget Sound.

Port Townsend, at the northeast corner of the peninsula, thrived at the turn of the century. It never became a major city but its carefully preserved and restored Victorian architecture is some of the best in the country. Fort Worden, constructed in 1897, has been designated a National Historic Landmark. To the west, Port Angeles is a gateway to the Olympics and is also a terminus for ferries to Victoria, British Columbia. A number of towns and villages west of here cater to the excellent salmon and halibut fishing of the Strait of Juan de Fuca.

The exposed northwest shore of the peninsula is marked by rocky windswept beaches and outcroppings, many accessible only to hikers. Further south, the highway parallels the coast as it passes through a portion of Olympic National Park. The strip of beach communities strung out along the broad sandy beaches north of Grays Harbor offer unparalleled sunsets and a chance to feast on the abundance of local clams. At the neck of the peninsula, connecting Hoquiam and Aberdeen on Grays Harbor with Olympia, is the less rugged southern end of the Olympic Mountains, with pleasant, easily accessible parks nearby.

Traditional method of smoking salmon.

Harbor, La Push.

Coastal sunset.

Constance Creek,
Dosewallips River area.

Historic Port Townsend.

Olympic National Park shoreline.

On the trail, Olympic National Park.

Hurricane Ridge,
Olympic National Park.

Naval ships near Whidbey Island.

*Tatoosh Lighthouse at the entrance to
Juan de Fuca Strait.*

The beginning of snow melt,
Olympic National Park.

Crabbing.

General store, Joyce, Washington,
on the Olympic Peninsula.

Rainforest, Hoh River area.

Discovery Bay.

Photo Credits

Walter Hodges/First Light pp. 44, 77

John D. Luke/First Light p. 53

Brian Milne/First Light p. 85

Warren Morgan/First Light p. 6

Jack Rogers pp. iii, 1, 5, 9, 10, 11, 12, 13, 14, 15, 16, 20, 21, 22, 23, 24, 27, 28, 29, 30, 31, 32, 36, 37, 39, 40, 41, 42, 43, 49, 50, 52, 55, 58, 59, 60, 63, 64, 65, 66, 67, 68, 69, 70, 71, 72, 75, 76, 78, 79, 80, 83, 86, 88, 89

Bill Ross/First Light pp. 2, 57, 81, 82

Robert Semniuk/First Light p. 87

Mark Stephenson/First Light p. 51

Ken Straiton/First Light p. 46

Ron Watts pp. 38, 45

Ron Watts/First Light p. 56

Doug Wilson p. 54

Doug Wilson/First Light p. 19

Michael Yamashita p. 84

Michael Burch p. 35